GW00500135

Contents

Foreword

As its title suggests, this book is a collection of many of the best-loved sacred solos. The voice part is intended primarily for sopranos or tenors, but many of the settings lie in the middle range of these voices and can equally well be sung by altos or basses.

Although some of the accompaniments are for the organ, the music has been arranged so that, with one or two minor adjustments, it may be played on the piano or any keyboard.

PIE JESU

Text: From the Requiem Mass
Music: Gabriel Fauré (1845-1924), arr. Alan Ridout

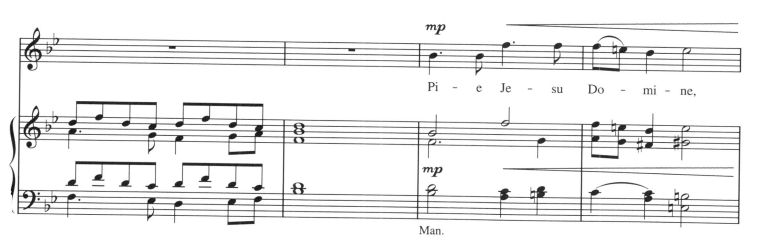

re - qui - em, sem - pi - ter - nam re - qui - em.

Pie, pi - e Je - su, pi - e Je - su Do - mi - ne,

do - na e - is, do - na e - is sem - pi - ter - nam

re - qui - em, sem - pi - ter - nam re - qui - em.

JESU, JOY OF MAN'S DESIRING

Text: Robert Bridges (1844-1930)
Music: Johann Sebastian Bach (1685-1750), arr. Alan Ridout

1. Je - su, joy of man's de - sir - ing,
2. Through the way where hope is guid - ing,

ho - ly wis - dom, love most
hark, what peace - ful mu - sic

Word of God, our
Theirs is beau - ty's

flesh that fa - shioned
fair - est plea - sure:

soar - ing, dy - ing, round thy throne.
in the love of joys un - known.

AVE VERUM CORPUS

Text: 14th century
Music: Wolfgang Amadeus Mozart (1756-1791)

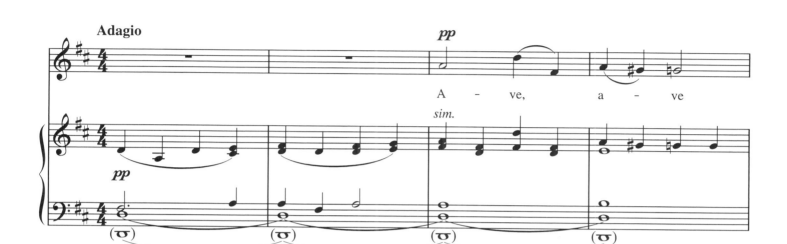

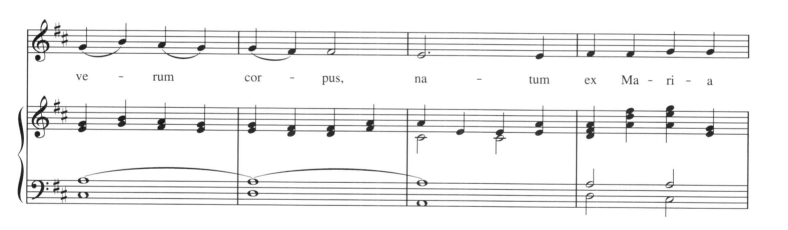

im - mo - la - tum in cru - ce pro ho - mi - ne.

Cu - jus la - tus per - fo - ra - tum un - da flux - it et san - gui -

Man.

PANIS ANGELICUS

Text: Thomas Aquinas (1227-1274)
Music: César Franck (1822-1890), arr. Alan Ridout

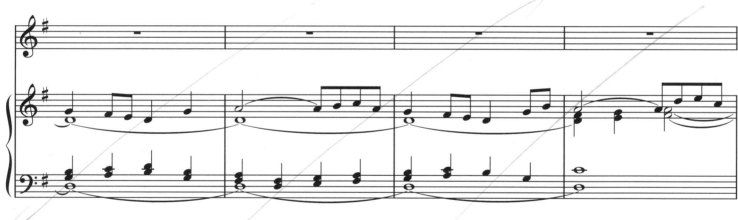

pau - per, pau - per, ser - vus et hu - mi - lis.

Man.

Pa - nis an - ge - li - cus fit pa - nis ho - mi - num,

Ped.

dat pa - nis coe - li - cus fi - gu - ris ter - mi - num:

AVE MARIA

Text: Luke 1
Music: adapted from J. S. Bach
by Charles Gounod (1818-1893)

ven - tris tu - i Je - sus.

cresc. poco a poco

Sanc - ta, Ma - ri - a, sanc - ta Ma-

cresc. poco a poco

f *p*

ri - a, Ma - ri - a! O - ra pro

f *pp*

cresc.

no - bis, no - bis pec - ca - to - ri - bus

cresc.

22

nunc   et   in   ho   -   ra, in ho   -   ra

mor - tis no - strae,   A   -   men,

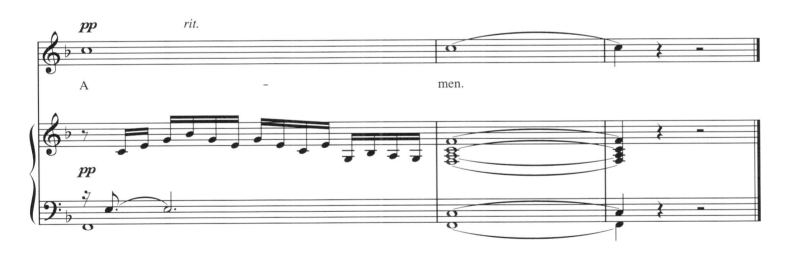

A   -   men.

BIST DU BEI MIR

Text: Michael Forster (b.1946)
Music: Johann Sebastian Bach (1685-1750), arr. Alan Ridout

with what con - tent - - ment I'll find in death my life's re -
pose, I'll find in death my life's re - pose. O sweet in -
deed would be my end - ing, if you, in
death my soul be - friend - ing, with gen - tle hands my eye - lids close.

O sweet in - deed would be my end - ing, if you, in death my soul be - friend - ing, with gen - tle hands my eye - lids close.

If you are here, with what con - tent - ment I'll find in death my life's re - pose, I'll find in death my life's re - pose

THE VIRGIN'S SLUMBER SONG

Text: Michael Forster (b.1946)
Music: Max Reger (1873-1916)

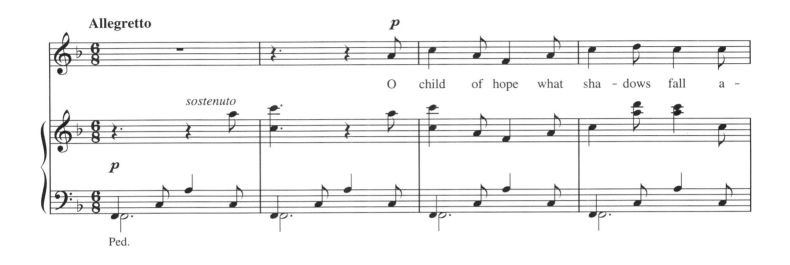

O child of pro - mise – such a cost, but such a prize!

O soft - ly slum - ber,

child of grace! Child of sor - row,

child of joy, child of mys - te - ry di - vine, may your peace - ful,

trust - ing sleep   be   of hope the   seal   and sign.

O   soft - ly   slum -   ber,

child   of   grace!

O FOR THE WINGS OF A DOVE

Text: Psalm 55: 6,7
Music: Felix Mendelssohn (1809-1847), arr. Alan Ridout

O for the wings, for the wings of a dove! Far a-way, far a-

way would I rove. O for the wings for the wings of a dove!

Far a-way, far a-way, far a-way, far a-way would I rove. In the

wil - der-ness build me a nest, and re - main there for e - ver at

rest in the wil - der - ness build me, build me a nest,

and re - main there for e - ver at rest, in the wil - der - ness

build me a nest, and re - main there for e - ver at rest.

And   re - main   there for   e   –   ver at rest,   and   re - main   there for

e   –   ver   at   rest.

BROTHER JAMES' AIR

Text: Psalm 23 from 'The Scottish Psalter' (1650)
Music: James Leith Macbeth Bain (c.1860-1925), arr. Alan Ridout

qui - et wa - ters   by.
staff me com - fort   still.

mp

2. My   soul he doth re - store a - gain, and   me to walk doth
4. My   ta - ble thou hast fur - ni - shed in   pre - sence of my

mf

make   with - in the paths of right-eous-ness, e'en   for his own name's
foes;   my   head thou dost with oil a - noint, and   my cup o - ver -

p

sake,   with - in the paths of right-eous-ness, e'en   for his own name's sake.
flows,   my   head thou dost with oil a - noint, and   my cup o - ver - flows.

Ped.

5. Good- ness and mer - cy all my life shall sure - ly fol - low me, and in God's house for e - ver-more my dwell -ing place shall be, and in God's house for e - ver-more my dwell -ing place shall be.

Man.

Ped.

rall.

O REST IN THE LORD

Text: Psalm 37
Music: Felix Mendelssohn (1809-1847), arr. Alan Ridout

O rest in the Lord, wait pa-tient-ly for him, and he shall

give thee thy heart's de - sires, O rest in the Lord, wait pa-tient-ly for

him, and he shall give thee thy heart's de - sires, and he shall

give thee thy heart's de - sires. Com - mit thy way un - to him, and trust in

Man.

him, com - mit thy way un - to him, and trust in him, and fret not thy -

Ped.

self be - cause of e - vil do - ers. O rest in the Lord, wait pa - tient - ly for

him, wait pa - tient - ly for him, O rest in the Lord, wait pa - tient - ly for

him, and he shall give thee thy heart's de - sires, and he shall

give thee thy heart's de - sires, and he shall give thee thy heart's de -

sires. O rest in the Lord, O rest in the Lord, and wait,

wait pa - tient - ly for him.

AVE MARIA

Text: Luke 1
Music: Franz Schubert (1797-1828)

na,   Ma - ri - a gra-ti-a ple - na,   Do-mi-nus te-
bis,   o - ra, o-ra pro no - bis   pec-ca-to - ri -

cum,   be - dic - ta tu in mu-li - e - ri-bus,   et
bus,   nunc et in ho - ra mor - tis no - strae,   in

be - ne - dic - tus,   et be - ne-dic-tus fruc-tus
ho - ra mor - tis no - strae,   nunc et in ho - ra mor - tis

ven - tris,   ven-tris tu - i, Je - sus.
no - strae,   in ho - ra mor - tis no - strae.

A - ve Ma - ri - a!
A - ve Ma - ri - a!

dim. al fine

I KNOW THAT MY REDEEMER LIVETH

Text: Job 19:25

Music: George Frideric Handel (1685-1759), arr. Alan Ridout

and that he shall stand at the lat - ter day up - on the earth.

I know that my Re -

deem – er liv – eth, and that he shall stand

at the lat – ter day up-on the earth,

up-on the earth. I know that my Re - deem - er

liv – eth, and he shall stand at the lat – ter day

up - on the earth, up - on the

earth.

mf

STEAL AWAY

Text: Spiritual
Music: Spiritual, arr. Colin Mawby

Steal a-way, steal a-way, steal a-way to Je - sus!

Steal a-way, steal a-way home, I ain't got long to stay here.

1. My Lord calls me, he calls me by the thun - der;
2. Green trees are bend - ing, poor sin - ners stand a - trem - bling, the
3. My Lord calls me, he calls me by the light - ning;

trum-pet sounds with-in-a my soul: I ain't got long to stay here. Steal a-way,

steal a-way, steal a-way to Je - sus! Steal a-way,

steal a-way home, I ain't got long to stay here. stay here.

SHEEP MAY SAFELY GRAZE

Text: Michael Forster (b.1946)
Music: Johann Sebastian Bach (1685-1750), arr. Alan Ridout

Sheep may safe - ly graze un - hin - dered with the faith - ful

shep - herd near. Sheep may safe - ly graze un - hin - dered,

(Man.)

sheep may safe - ly graze un - hin - dered,

with the faith - ful shep - herd near, with the

faith - ful shep - herd near.

2nd time only

2nd time only

(Ped.)

Where the lea - ders of the na - tions seek the heal - ing

of cre - a - tion, peace will put an end to fear.

(Man.)

50

Where the lea - ders of the na - tions seek the heal - ing of cre - a - tion, seek the heal - ing of cre - a - tion peace will put, will put an end to fear.

rit.

D.C.

AVE MARIA

Text: Luke 1
Music: Giulio Caccini (c.1545-1618), arr. Christopher Tambling

ri - a.   A - - - - - ve.

a - - - - - - - - - - ve.

rit.

HE SHALL FEED HIS FLOCK

Text: Isaiah 40:11; Matthew 11: 28, 29
Music: George Frideric Handel (1685-1759), arr. Colin Hand

shep - herd, and he shall ga - ther the lambs with his arm,

with his arm, and car - ry them

in his bo - som, and gen - tly lead those that are with young, and

gen - tly lead those, and gen - tly lead those that are with young.

he will give you rest. Take his yoke up-on you, and

learn of him, for he is meek and low - ly of heart, and

ye shall find rest, and ye shall find rest un - to your souls.

Take his yoke up-on you, and learn of him, for

60

he is meek and low - ly of heart, and ye shall find rest, and

ye shall find rest un - to your souls.

NOBODY KNOWS THE TROUBLE I'VE SEEN

Text: Spiritual
Music: Spiritual, arr. Christopher Tambling

Unaccompanied first time only

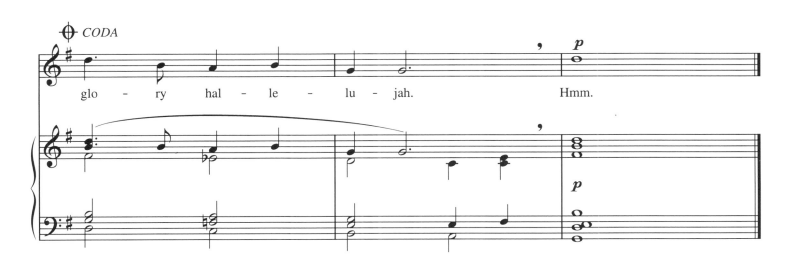

LEAD ME, LORD

Text: Psalm 5:8; 4:8
Music: Samuel Sebastian Wesley (1810-1876)

right - eous - ness, make thy way plain be - fore my face.

Man.

For it is thou, Lord, thou, Lord, on - ly, that mak - est me

dwell in safe - ty. For it is thou, Lord,

p

Ped.

thou, Lord, on - ly, that mak - est me dwell in safe - ty.

p *rit.*

rit.

p

SWING LOW, SWEET CHARIOT

Text: Sarah Hannah Sheppard
Music: Sarah Hannah Sheppard, arr. Colin Mawby

Swing low, sweet cha - ri - ot, com - ing for to car - ry me home; swing low, sweet cha - ri - ot, com - ing for to car - ry me home.

1. I looked o - ver Jor - dan, and what did I see, com - ing for to car - ry me

(3.) some - times up, I'm some - times down, com - ing for to car - ry me

home? A band of an-gels com-ing af-ter me, com-ing for to car-ry me
home: but still my soul feels hea-ven-ly bound, com-ing for to car-ry me

home. Swing low, sweet cha - ri - ot, com-ing for to car-ry me

2nd time rit.

home; swing low, sweet cha - ri - ot, com-ing for to car-ry me

1. **2.** *Fine*

home. 2. If home. (2.) you get there be - fore I do,

coming for to car-ry me home; tell all my friends I'm com-ing too,

coming for to car-ry me home; swing low, sweet cha - ri - ot,

coming for to car-ry me home, swing low, sweet

cha - ri - ot, com-ing for to car-ry me home. 3. I'm

D.S. al Fine

THE HEAVENS ARE TELLING

Text: Psalm 19:1-4
Music: Franz Joseph Haydn (1732-1809), arr. Colin Hand

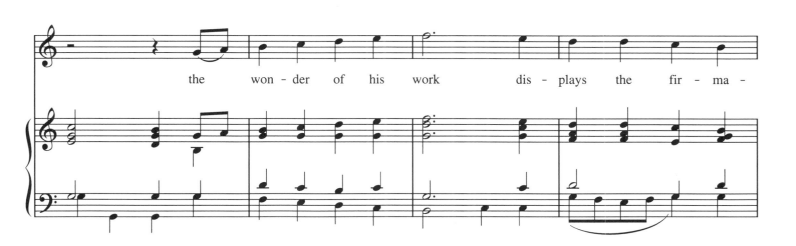

ment, the won - der of his

work dis - plays the fir - ma - ment.

To - day that is

com - ing speaks it the day;

work, the won- der of his work dis- plays the fir- ma-

ment, in all the lands re- sounds the

word, ne- ver un- per- cei- ved, e- ver un- der-

stood, e- ver, e- ver, e- ver

un - der - stood, e - ver, e - ver,

e - ver, e - ver un - der -

stood. The hea - vens are tell - ing the glo - ry of

God, the won - der of his work, the

won - der of his work dis - plays, dis - plays the

fir - ma - ment, dis - plays the fir - ma - ment, dis -

plays the fir - ma - ment.

LAUDATE DOMINUM

Text: Psalm 117
Music: Wolfgang Amadeus Mozart (1756-1791)

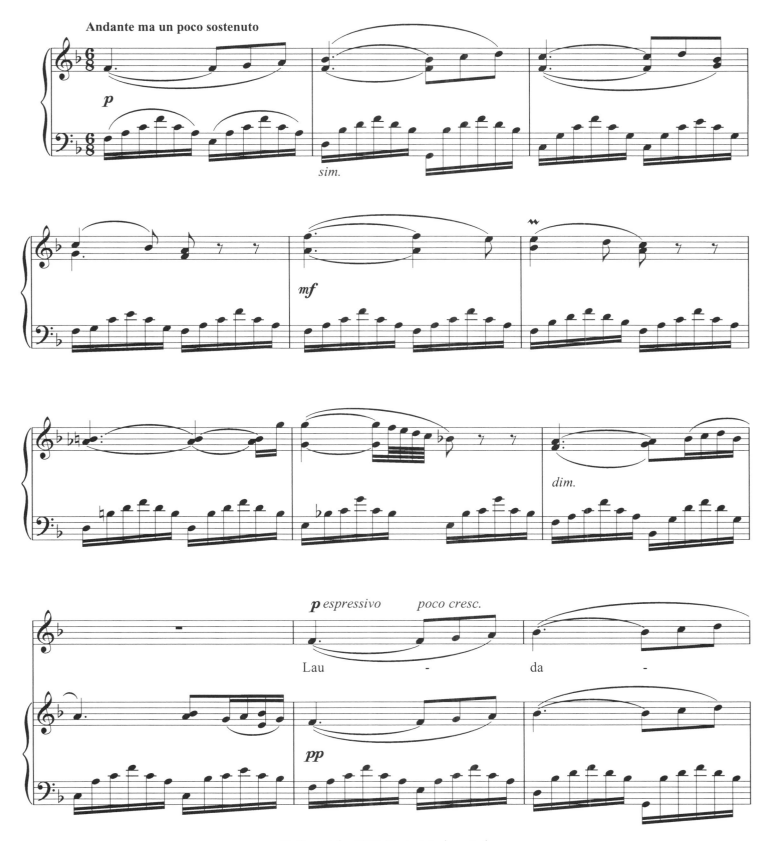

quo - ni - am con - fir - ma - ta est   su -   per____

nos_____ mi - se - ri - cor - di - a

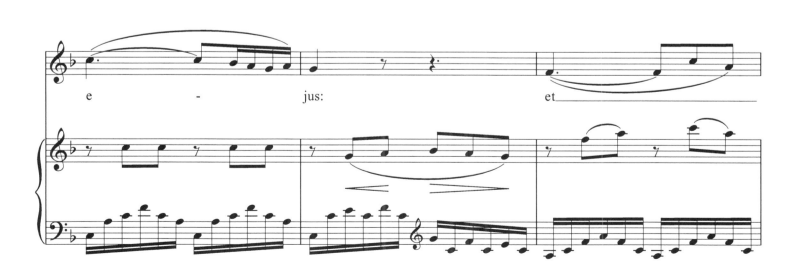

e -   jus: et_____

ve - ri -tas, ve - ri - tas Do - mi - ni

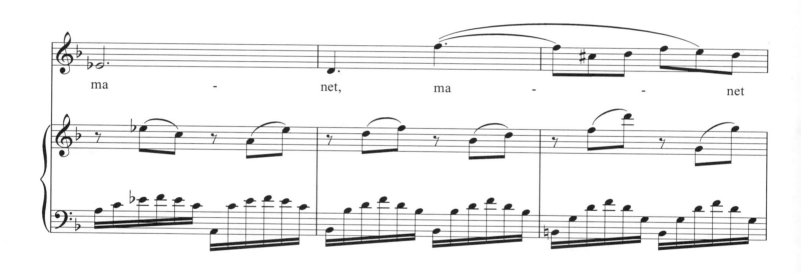

ma - net, ma - net

in_____ ae - ter - num. A -

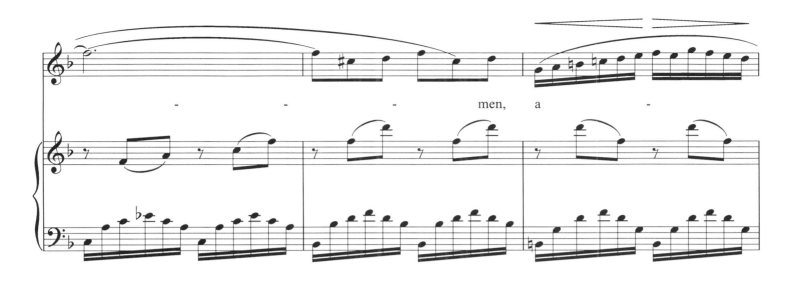